Scars

Yorkshire Publishing
TULSA

ISBN: 978-1-960810-42-7
Scars

Copyright © 2024 by Marina Murray
All rights reserved.

No part of this publication may be reproduced, distributed, or transmitted in any form or by any means, including photocopying, recording, or other electronic or mechanical methods, without the prior written permission of the publisher, except in the case of brief quotations embodied in critical reviews and certain other noncommercial uses permitted by copyright law.

For permission requests, write to the publisher at the address below.

Yorkshire Publishing
1425 E 41st Pl
Tulsa, OK 74105
www.YorkshirePublishing.com
918.394.2665

Published in the USA

Scars

Marina Murray

CONTENT WARNING: This book explores aspects of domestic violence and domestic abuse. Please read with caution.

If you or someone that you know is experiencing domestic violence, you can contact the National Domestic Violence Hotline: 1-800-799-SAFE or visit thehotline.org.

Contents

Dismantling the Lies 9	Goodbye 43	Solo................................72
Masterpiece on Display ..12	Sorry Not Sorry..............44	I Win 73
I Let You Down..............13	Forgotten Secrets............45	Sunrise 74
Just Like Him.................14	Imperfections 46	You'll Love It 75
Nothing to Gain.............15	Guarded 47	Lazy Days.......................76
I Miss Him.....................16	Know My Soul 48	Free 77
Just in Case 17	Glad You're Gone 49	Falling in Love...............78
Breaking the Rules..........18	Let Go............................50	Favorite Adventure 79
Broken 20	Solitude..........................51	Waiting 80
I Never Got it Right.......21	Alone 52	Shy..................................81
Songs of My Heart 22	Lonely 53	What's Your Story...........82
Scars...............................23	I Hate This.....................54	Mini Adventure..............83
Silenced Voice 24	Blooming 55	Christian Too 84
Pretty Lies 25	Help Me Grow...............56	Where You Are 85
Help................................26	Beauty 57	You Love Me 86
Carry Me........................27	Broken Pieces 58	Love 87
My Hero of War.............28	Songs of the Soul............59	Heart Beat......................88
Shhhh… 30	Boundaries 60	Home Sick 89
Escape 31	Teach Me 61	Come On.......................90
The Courage to Go 32	Identity in Christ 62	Join Me 91
I'll Find Me 33	Rest in You 63	Him 92
Take My Hand 34	Everything......................64	The Best.........................93
Fear.................................35	Your Way........................65	Be My Rock 94
I'll Trust You...................36	I Need You Everyday 66	Lost with You 95
Mysterious Freedom.......37	Let's Go..........................67	Someplace with You 96
Second Chance...............38	I'm Yours........................68	You.................................97
You Care 39	In Love with You............69	A Moment with You.......98
Confused........................41	Food for the Soul 70	Your Song.......................99
Finding Peace 42	I Trust You 71	Dear Future Husband ..100

To share this part of my life is a great challenge for me. However, I want to share my story because there are so many silent victims of domestic violence. God never gave me a spirit of fear, but one of love, power, and of a sound mind. I am tired of allowing my voice to be silenced by fear, so today, I am choosing to speak up and speak out. My hope is that my story helps encourage someone else to set themselves free.

–Marina

Dismantling the Lies

There were many lies that I believed which kept me in an abusive relationship. As a Christian, I was taught that divorce without biblical grounds is a sin, and the only biblical grounds for divorce is adultery. I want to argue that domestic violence is also biblical grounds for divorce. Marriage may be difficult at times, but it is not a curse or a trap; it is a tremendous blessing. God called husbands to love their wives in the way that Christ loved the church. Meaning that husbands are called to love and to sacrifice themselves for their wives just like Jesus loved and sacrificed himself for the church. Wives are called to submit to their husbands. This does not mean that they are servants, slaves, or lesser beings. It simply means that we wives need to let our husbands be the leaders of our homes. It is true that God hates divorce. The reason that God hates divorce is because divorce is caused by sin, and it causes pain and destruction of relationships. God does not hate divorced people; God hates the action of divorce. God hates the sin, not the sinner. Malachi 2:16 says, "…To divorce your wife is to overwhelm her with cruelty… so guard your heart and do not be unfaithful to your wife." Colossians 3:19 says, "Husbands love your wives, and never treat them harshly." 1 Peter 3:7 says, "In the same way, you husbands must give honor to your wives. Treat your wife with understanding as you live together. She may be weaker than you are, but she is your equal partner in God's gift of new life. Treat her as you should so your prayers will not be hindered." These are God's commands (instructions) for a husband. A spouse who fails to follow these components of the marriage covenant is violating the marriage vows. Chronic and repeated abuse is not loving your wife as Christ loved the church; it is treating her harshly. Abuse in any form does not give honor or provide understanding to a wife; these actions violate the marriage covenant. These biblical instructions make it very clear that God does not tolerate the abuse or mistreatment of wives. If a husband refuses to follow God's commands for a marriage, how can a Christian wife be expected to stay? In 1 Corinthians 5:9-11, Paul rebukes (corrects) the church. Paul informs the church that they are not supposed to associate with people who claim to be a Christian but continue to indulge in sin. In the list of sins that Paul lists in the New Living Translation is the word "abusive." Now, when Paul says the word abusive, he does not limit it to one form of abuse because all forms of abuse are sinful (physical, verbal, sexual, etc.). Paul just says the word abusive, which we can assume means all forms of abuse. In 1 Corinthians 6:9-11 Paul says that some believers were once like that, but they were cleansed and made holy by calling on the name of the Lord Jesus Christ and by the Holy Spirit. Paul says that people who continue to indulge in these sins yet claim to be a believer will not inherit the Kingdom of God (Heaven). The Kingdom of God is reserved for followers of Christ. In 1 Corinthians, Paul suggests that despite these peoples' claims to be Christian, if they continue to indulge in the sins listed in 1 Corinthians 5:9-11, which includes abuse, they are not truly Christians or followers of Christ. God does not call anyone to live in an abusive marriage or to tolerate mistreatment. That simply is not the nature of God. God's nature is one of peace, mercy, grace, and love. There is no love in abuse. An earthly father would be angered to know that his daughter is being abused. So, how much more does it anger your heavenly father? Psalms 9:9 says, "The Lord is a shelter for the oppressed, a refuge in times of trouble." Psalms 103:6 "The Lord gives righteousness and justice to all who are treated unfairly." Psalm 75:10 "For God says, "I will break the strength of the wicked, but I will increase the power of the godly."" Do not allow yourself to stay and be abused. Please have the courage to leave and put your hope and trust in God.

Marina Murray

Masterpiece on Display

Each poem is a gentle whisper of
the wounds upon my soul.
Each line, revealing a scar.
As you read, you're running your finger
across the scars upon my heart.
Poetry is the language that my soul speaks.
It's riddles and mysteries gently revealing my pain.
Come, be entertained by the grieving of my soul.
It is through these gentle whispers that
my heartaches are revealed.
Cloaked in mystery, and as gentle as a breeze,
it is through poetry that my soul sings.
Close your eyes and listen to the song of my soul,
for there is beauty in my pain.
This beauty is not found in perfection,
but in the unique wounds and scars that my heart holds.
No scar is the same.
Come marvel at my pain.
It is a masterpiece on display.

Scars

I Let You Down

I messed up tonight.
That look in your eyes means that
there is gonna be a fight.
Crippled by fear, I don't know what to say.
I am sure that it is my fault, that you had a bad day.
How did I mess up now?
I never left the house,
and when we watched your show,
I was as silent as a mouse.
I did everything that you asked.
I completed every task.
My heart pounds as though it will come out of my chest.
Your voice is so loud, I can't make out all of the words.
Pinned against the wall, I am too afraid to fight.
All I know is that there is something that I didn't do right.
I close my eyes to soften the blow.
Praying for the moment that you'll let me go.
I try so hard to be perfect, but I never get it right.
I'm sorry that I let you down again tonight.
I wish that I was a better wife.
Maybe one day, I'll get things right.

Marina Murray

Just Like Him

Your heart filled with anger, pain, and shame
It was with me that you tried to find blame
Your anger was something that you couldn't tame
Your father was exactly the same

Scars

Nothing to Gain

Your heart filled with secrets that you won't say
You ruminate on them night and day
You turn to alcohol to numb your pain
You grip your secrets tightly, as though
through it, you'll find something to gain
Something triggered a secret memory,
and you went into a fit of rage
Making me feel hopelessly trapped inside a cage

Marina Murray

I Miss Him

I begin to wither and wilt
As you strip away the joy from my life
I often wonder what happened to the man that I married
He was sweet, gentle, and kind
It was his arms that once made me feel safe and secure
He kissed me softly
He was so gentle and sweet
I miss him each and every day

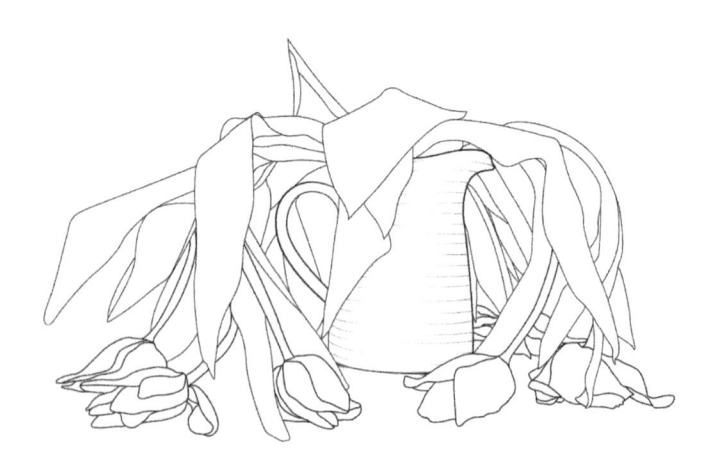

Just in Case

I text my mom that I love her
I hope that she doesn't know why
But I texted my mom that I love her because,
I'm afraid that I'll die

Marina Murray

Breaking the Rules

I snuck out today
It's not allowed, but I did it anyway
I can't leave without you
You accompany me in all that I do
You're afraid that I'll slip up and say
That you punish me each day
You grip my arm tightly when I speak too much
It's your subtle way of telling me to hush
My heart sinks when we walk to the car
Because I accidentally went too far
I smile and wave goodbye
I try not to cry
As soon as we are out of sight
You start my punishment for the night
Tonight's will be worse, I know
Because I had the courage to go
I saw my family today
I didn't slip up and say
Anything about how you punish me each day
Or that I can't leave unless you say
My punishment will be severe, I know
I just really wanted to go
I silently walk into the house
Trying to be as quiet as a mouse
You see me and chase me up the stairs
I often feel as though nobody cares
I choke back tears and die inside
There is no place for me to run or hide

Scars

I asked for help, but I was told to stay
Despite my concern, they told you about it anyway
I'm trapped, and I can't get out
My hope has been replaced with doubt
My God, I am trapped. I don't know what to do
My soul silently cries out to You

Marina Murray

Broken

Lord, please hold my heart.
It hurts too much inside my chest.

Scars

I Never Got it Right

The loud screams of silence echo through the halls.
I'm lost in the silence; nothing is the same,
Now that you're not around, there's no one
to tell me what to do, think, or wear.
Your strict rules were only because you care.
This silence overwhelms me; it's far too loud.
I no longer hear your screams, breaking
dishes, or stomping up the stairs.
My bruises and scars are proof of how much you care.
I should have known better than to ask for your help.
I'm sorry that your beers were too warm.
Sometimes, I forgot to ask for your
permission before I left the house.
I'm sorry that I didn't fold your clothes the right way.
I forgot to ask you before I bought that pair of shoes.
I'm so forgetful, I don't remember all of the rules.
I always seem to let you down.
Maybe that's why you are no longer around.
I tried my best to be a good wife,
I'm sorry that I never got it right.

Songs of My Heart

Jesus, you're the song of my heart
Even when my world falls apart
You're The One that I cling to
I will always put my hope and trust in You

Scars

The scars are still there
They're the proof of how much you care
Over time, they've lost their sting and pain
But every word that you screamed at me in vain
Cut deeper than a knife
I'm your ex-wife
Who never got things right
You'd scold me every night
Every word would bite
You never let me out of your sight

Silenced Voice

"Things are great," I say
My voice trembles as I choke on that lie
I don't dare speak the truth
I feel him reach for my hand
"She's shy," he says with a grin
He takes over answering questions now
Once again, my voice is hushed
I can't be left to speak too much
I might reveal a secret that I can't say
So, he does all of the talking again today

Scars

Pretty Lies
....

Painted lips and fancy speech,
help disguise the truth behind her words

Marina Murray

Help

Afraid to leave and afraid to stay,
God, please lead the way.

Scars

Carry Me

Please carry me, Lord,
because today,
I have no strength.

Marina Murray

My Hero of War

We praise and thank our veterans for their
service when they return from war.
We smile and wave at them in the parades.
They're the American Heroes who survived the fight.
But their battle still wages on,
their home has become the battlefield now.
You must walk on eggshells to survive.
We military wives just try to make it through the day.
Be careful not to make a loud or unexpected sound.
They are on guard and ready to fight
Sometimes, they attack in the middle of the night
Concealer helps disguise the bruises;
sunglasses hide our puffy eyes.
Long-sleeved shirts cover the marks on our arms.
These superficial wounds are easy to hide.
The greatest wounds we wives bear
are the ones that go unseen.
When the veterans return home, their war
is over, but ours has just begun.
Tucked behind our lipsticked smiles is
a secret that we don't dare say.
We can't slander these heroes of war,
We just know that they like to slam the door.
They prefer liquor to numb their pain.
Their repeated stories are all the same,
nod and pretend to be engaged.
Otherwise, he might go into a fit of rage.
Us military wives are strong,

Scars

We survived the fight,
but it is time for me to close this chapter of my life.
Goodbye, my hero of war,
I won't be there to hear you slam the door.
I don't need concealer to cover my eyes.
Long-sleeved shirts are no longer my disguise.
I've somehow managed to overcome this pain,
Maybe one day, you'll do the same.

Shhhh...

I tear my heart apart
to reveal the secrets that are hidden inside.

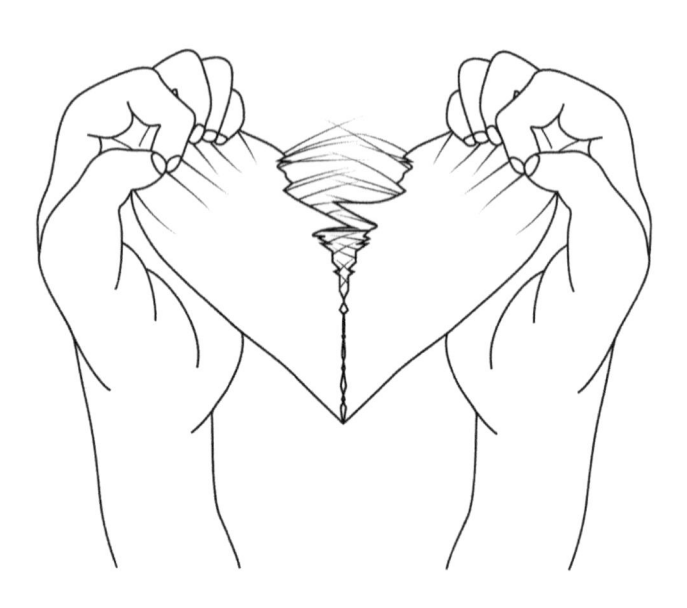

Escape

....

I rush to leave,
I feel the strain and breaking of my back.
I'm in a rush to leave,
because I'm never going back.

Marina Murray

The Courage to Go

Men that are boozed,
Who leave their wives battered and bruise
This was not God's calling for your life
God did not intend for husbands to be
filled with anger, bitterness, and strife
Women whose voices are silenced by fear
Just know that God is near
Call upon the name of the Lord, He will set you free
I know because He did it for me
Women, violence was not God's calling for your life
Victim of abuse is not the role of a wife
Abused wives, I encourage you to flee
Men trapped in the cycle of abuse
The devil put this chain around your neck like a noose
Have the courage to break the cycle today
Men surrender to Jesus and pray
God has seen it all
Wait patiently for His call
There is still purpose for your life
It has nothing to do with anger, bitterness, or strife
From the lips of a battered ex-wife,
God has a great purpose for your life
Pack your bags today
Cry out to Jesus and pray
God has a great plan for your life
Enduring violence was never God's calling for a wife
God loves you more than you can know
Please have the courage to go

Scars

I'll Find Me

Navigating this new freedom is challenging to do.
I am so used to being under the strict control of you.
You determined what I should wear, go, and do.
This freedom of independence is so new.
I feel overwhelmed with the freedom to choose.
Lost in the options, I feel like it's a battle that I'll lose.
For so long, you silenced my voice.
Now, I meticulously calculate every thought and choice
Afraid that I'll somehow make a mistake
Small decisions often feel too difficult to make
I no longer know who I am anymore
You controlled me to the very core
You stripped away every piece of myself
I'm hopelessly searching for these pieces
like they are lost on a shelf
How do I go back to being me
I feel like I am lost at sea
I'm lost in an ocean of decisions that
feel impossible to make.
I no longer know who I am; I feel like a phony or a fake.
I no longer know what I like to wear.
I know that you don't really care,
But I miss the young woman that I used to be.
I'm learning how to cope with this new version of me.
Some days, it feels too difficult
to be free.
I'm overwhelmed, trying to figure out who to be.
Maybe one day, I'll find me.

Marina Murray

Take My Hand

I share my story to extend my hand and pull you out
Don't let his words fill your heart with
fear, hopelessness, and doubt
You are powerful, beautiful, and strong
His actions are wrong
Nothing can justify his mistreatment of you
And don't underestimate what Jesus can do
Call upon the name of the Lord, He will set you free
I know because He did it for me

Fear

I am so tired of being afraid
The fear of you silences my voice
I am afraid to be found
You controlled me every day
Even still, you try to restrict what I say
Sometimes, I wonder if I am truly free
Because I still have this fear
that one day, you'll find me

Marina Murray

I'll Trust You

Through the fire and the flames,
    Your love still remains.
    So, I'll trust You Lord.

Mysterious Freedom

Sometimes, it's hard knowing who I am supposed to be.
Remembering how to let myself get lost and free
is an old mystery.

Marina Murray

Second Chance

I don't know how to be alone.
It's hard to know what to wear.
What am I supposed to do?
Where am I supposed to go?
Meticulously calculating every thought, it's
hard to know what's wrong or right.
Sometimes, it is hard being out of your sight.
As challenging and confusing as it may be,
I love this new victory.
This newfound freedom permeates my soul.
I look to Jesus to make me whole.
I am not perfect, I still make mistakes,
But I never have to hear the dishes break
I no longer see your holes in the wall
I don't have to run and hide
You're no longer glued to my side
I grow stronger each day
You tried to crush my spirit and break my soul
Through Jesus, I'll be made whole
Despite the bitterness and pain
And all that you have said and done in vain
Jesus set me free
He put joy in my soul
Every day, I sing His praises and dance
Because Jesus gave me a second chance.

Scars

You Care

....

I am cloaked in despair
Left wondering if You care
My soul is grieved by the misfortunes of life
The pain cuts deeper than a knife
Medicine cannot heal the wounds of my soul
These troubles made my heart blacker than coal
My spirit is colder than the night
There is no hope for me left in sight
But it is in the power of Your might
That I have been brought to the light
Your words heal the wounds of my soul
It is through You that I have been made whole
Your light shines so bright
It can be seen on the darkest night
You healed the wounds of my heart
And from me, You promised never to part
You brought me peace when I was in despair
Each day, You remind me that You care
You give me joy despite this pain
Your actions are never done in vain
You catch every tear
And remind me not to fear
You stand by my side
You'll never run or hide
You are mighty, powerful, and strong
And You are never wrong
You are stronger than any enemy weapon or foe
So, it is with You that I will always go

Your wisdom is so great
You have forever changed my fate
I will forever praise Your name
Knowing You is greater than any riches or fame
It's an honor to know the Lord
With Him, I'll never be bored
He heals and renews my mind and soul each day
I will never go astray
My God, I am pleased to serve You each day
You're the one that my soul will trust and obey
Your words are the medicine that soothes my soul
To glorify You is my life's goal
When problems come my way
I know that You'll always stay
You protect and comfort me when I am in need
Your faithfulness has nothing to do
with a good or bad deed
My God, please lead the way
I'll follow You every night and every day

Scars

Confused

I spent so much time trying to survive,
I've forgotten how to let myself live.

Marina Murray

Finding Peace

Finding comfort in the silence,
is easier than it was in your screams.

Scars

Goodbye
....

I am glad that you're gone
but, I miss the you that I thought that you were.

Marina Murray

Sorry Not Sorry
....

The peaceful silence of being alone,
is better than getting lost in the sea of your empty words.

Forgotten Secrets

The spoken truth is so taboo,
but, the memory of you is my favorite secret to forget.

Marina Murray

Imperfections

There's a beauty in the adornment of jagged pieces.
The rough edges of imperfection are
more attractive to the eye.

Scars

Guarded

My heart is too soft so,
I guard it with thorns.

Marina Murray

Know My Soul

You think that you know my soul because
you read it's fragments on a page
Which revealed pieces of its old cage
That's not who I am, just where I've been
You can read about it from the ink of my pen

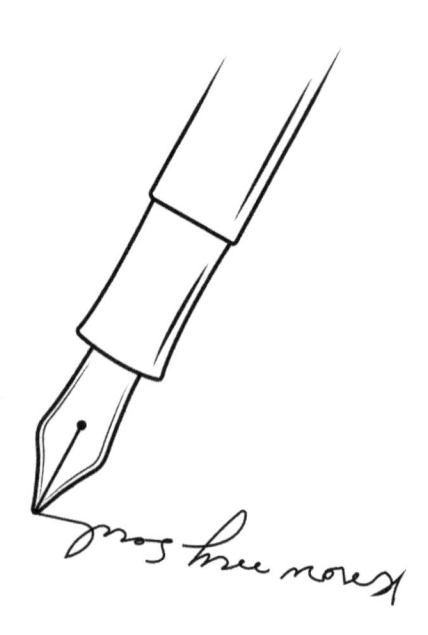

Glad You're Gone

Ever since I walked away
I get stronger each day
I am finding my voice,
And enjoying my choice.
I like jeans with ripped knees,
And V-necks and fitted tees.
My favorite color is green, but I like to wear red
I'm no longer filled with dread
You used to order me around
But to you, I am no longer bound
I no longer feel pressured to look like other girls
Now, I get to embrace my curls
I'm learning how to be me
This feeling is so free
I don't care what you said
To me, your opinion is dead
I get to be myself
I'm dusting off the pieces on the shelf
I wasn't lost for long
Freedom is my song
I'm no longer under the strict control of you
Now, I can choose what I wear, go, and do

Marina Murray

Let Go

You are so cruel
With an iron fist, is how you choose to rule
For so long, I lived in fear
I'm so glad that you're no longer here
It's easy for me to hate you
For all the things that you'd say and do
And let my heart grow bitter and vain
But from hatred, I have nothing to gain
I choose to let go, move on, forgive
With peace and joy is how I choose to live
Each day, I choose to be kind
And joy is what I find
I hope that one day you'll do the same
And your anger is something that you'll learn to tame

Solitude

Kissed by silence,
and hugged by empty space.
Solitude has become my favorite place.

Marina Murray

Alone

My favorite part about being alone,
is that it's a place that you'll never be.

Lonely

It's refreshing at times to do things by yourself,
but no one likes to feel alone.

Marina Murray

I Hate This

In the story of my life, this is not my favorite chapter.
God, can we skip ahead to the good part,
where my life is filled with joy and laughter.

Blooming

Sometimes, I wish that I could skip this part of my story but pain is where beauty thrives.

Marina Murray

Help Me Grow

You're so easy to hate
Because you're the monster that caused this fate
You're the one that caused this pain
You're so evil and vain
Forever, I want to hold you prisoner in my heart
God unleash every weapon and fiery dart!
It doesn't actually work this way
God has the final say
He loves you just as much as me
His heart breaks in ways that I'll never see
God has forgiven me of so many sins
With unforgiveness, nobody wins
God, help me let go
So that the love inside my heart can grow

Beauty

Maybe you'll find a unique beauty in my scars,
and I'll find a healing for these wounds.

Marina Murray

Broken Pieces

....

You tried to use your power to break me, but God makes my broken pieces shine. He's the master craftsman that illuminates the broken pieces that you left behind. I trust in Him and surrender the broken pieces of my heart. He wipes my tears and takes the pieces into His hands. He doesn't glue them back together, in an attempt to make me the same. Instead, He uses my broken pieces to create something beautiful, and uniquely its own, something the world hasn't seen.

Songs of the Soul

Sad songs are the ones that my soul likes to sing.
Sorrow and despair are the songs of my soul
but, I'm hoping soon to change the tune.

Marina Murray

Boundaries

I used to shrink so that you could grow,
but I have fallen in love with the word "no."

Teach Me

Lord, please dismantle the lies that I believe.
So, that I can learn to see myself the way that You see me.

Marina Murray

Identity in Christ

I am loved and valued by You. I am beautiful.
I was made in Your image. You have a plan and
purpose for my life. Some days, these simple truths
are hard to believe. I sometimes wonder how
You could love an imperfect person like me.

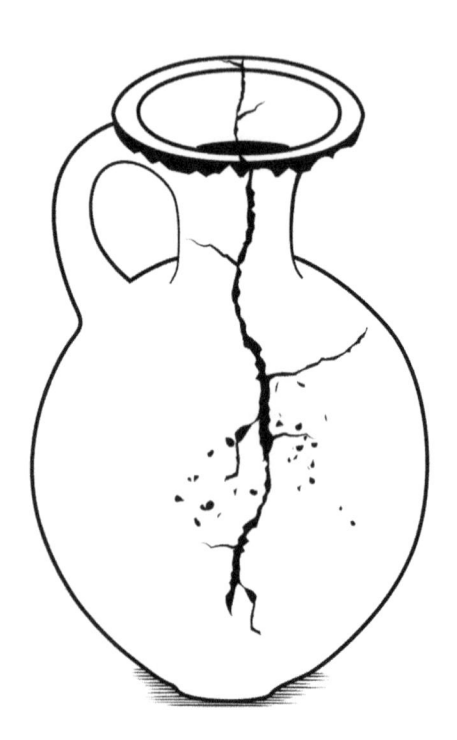

Rest in You

The comfort of Your promises, is the peace that I rest in.
When my soul is weary, and I feel faint,
it's in You that I find strength.

Marina Murray

Everything

God is woven into every fiber of my soul.
He will always be a part of everything that I do.

Scars

Your Way

Battered and bruised by this life
My heart doesn't choose bitterness or strife
When my soul is grieved and in despair
I call upon God, because I know that He will care
He listens to my soul grieve
He promised never to leave
Each day, He holds my hand
His blessings are so grand
Jesus, be the leader of my heart
From your ways, I will never part

Marina Murray

I Need You Everyday

Even on the toughest days,
I feel the warmth of your embrace.
Thank you for giving me the strength that I need today.
My God, with You, I'll always stay.

Let's Go

Our journey and relationship with God are
often referred to as our "walk with God."
but I told Him that I didn't want us
to walk; I want us to run.

Marina Murray

I'm Yours

Immerse me in You,
and catch every tear.
I belong to You
so, whom shall I fear.

In Love with You

Oh, how I fall in love with You more each day
I love to pray
It is a great honor to come before the Lord
Your strength is greater than any weapon or sword
You desire mercy, not sacrifice
It is Jesus who paid our price
I have been immersed in Your love
That You generously shower from above
Your word is a savory meat for my soul
I feast upon it daily, for you make me whole
You're the one that my soul chases after
You fill my heart with joy and laughter
You make me glad inside
From You, I'll never run or hide
In serving You, I take great pride
The Holy Spirit is my compass and spiritual guide
Lord, lead the way
Every night and day
I will follow You through the adventure of life
Your words are true, and Your wisdom
is sharper than a knife
To You, I surrender it all
I quietly wait for Your call
I am honored to serve You each day
From You, I will never go astray

Marina Murray

Food for the Soul

His word is the savory meat for my soul,
    and the healing to my wounds.

I Trust You

Overwhelmed with stress
You're readying me for the next step
I need to stretch and grow
Sometimes, I just want to go slow
But I trust Your plan
So, I hold out my hand
Lead the way
It's with You, that I'll always stay
I get on my knees to pray
Please, God, give me the strength that I need today

Marina Murray

Solo

Taking solo trips that were meant for two
Is slowly getting easier to do
Sometimes solo trips are fun
Even if they are only enjoyed by one

I Win

I dig my toes in the sand
Wondering how life can be so grand
I love the sound of the sea
The ocean makes me feel free
With sun-kissed skin and a grin
I smile because I win
I no longer live in fear
Because you are no longer near

Marina Murray

Sunrise

Crowned with curls and adventure in my eyes,
I'm getting lost in this sunrise.

You'll Love It

Riding motorcycles is so much fun
It's my favorite way to get some sun
I can ride for hours on end
I like to lean as I go around the bend
I love the sound that my engine makes
And the fresh, cool breeze as I drive around the lakes
What a joy to get lost on a back road
Us bikers wear leather, it's part of our code
The wind in my face makes me feel free
It's amazing all of the sights that you can see
The gasoline, the leather, the boots, and the gear
Us biker girls don't have fear
Sometimes, I rev my engine a little loud
Shifting into the next gear makes me
feel like I am floating on a cloud
Flying through the gears makes my heart race
It's a feeling that I love and embrace
Riding motorcycles is a great way to feel free
I'm sure that you'll love it just as much as me

Marina Murray

Lazy Days

Sitting on a bench soaking up the sun.
Long walks on lazy days are so much fun.

Free

Late-night gazes at the stars
Chirping crickets and fireflies
Enjoying this moment alone is fine with me
This peaceful moment reminds me that I am free

Marina Murray

Falling in Love
....

Remembering how to fall in love is harder than it seems. Not all things are easy to do but, it will come easily when I find you.

Favorite Adventure

My favorite adventure will be
the one that leads me to you.

Marina Murray

Waiting
....

While I wait for you
I'll blow you kisses beneath the stars
By the light of the moon

Shy

I saw you and fell in love with your smile,
But my shoes caught my grin.

Marina Murray

What's Your Story

Late-night picnics and gazing at the stars,
tell me the stories behind your scars.

Scars

Mini Adventure
....

A full tank of gas, and coffee for two,
I'm ready for a mini adventure with you.

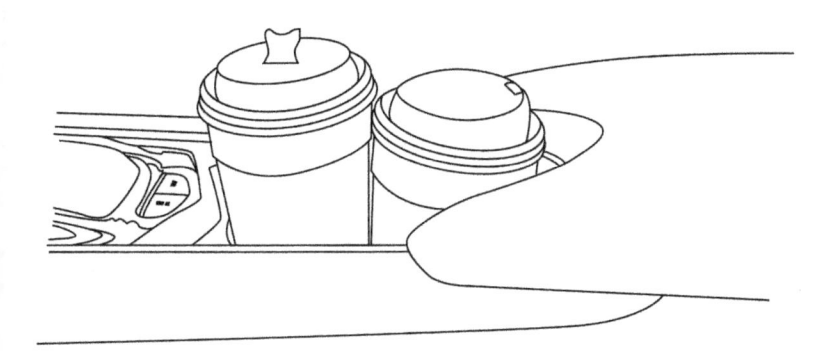

Marina Murray

Christian Too

My favorite thing about you,
Is that your heart carries a piece of Him too.

Where You Are

I'm in the car
Wishing on a star
Wondering where you are
I hope that God hasn't placed you far
Can I get there by car
Maybe one day He'll show me where you are

Marina Murray

You Love Me

You'll tell me that you love me
Without a secret motive in mind
You'll tell me that you love me
Because your words are kind

Love

Love songs resonate so deeply with us all
Because we long for the wholeness of His love.

Marina Murray

Heart Beat

When my heart skipped a beat,
its rhythm matched yours.

Scars

Home Sick

This night is the best
I rest my head on your chest
The perfect evening for two
This is when my heart first fell in love with you
I "borrowed" your sweater, I thought that you knew
It's for days like these when I'm homesick for you

Marina Murray

Come On

Let's go to the beach or a park
Or maybe we can look at art
I don't really care
As long as you are there
These small moments are fun to share

Join Me

Join me on the river,
The water is high, and the weather is great
Join me on the river,
I'm excited; don't make me wait
Join me on the river,
Bring a kayak with you
Join me on the river,
It's the perfect adventure for two

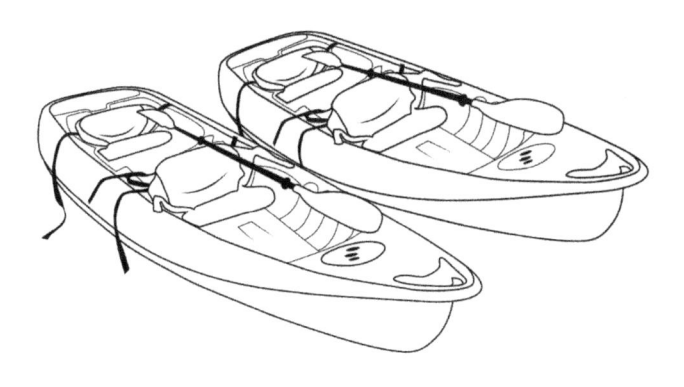

Marina Murray

Him

....

Your arms will be my safe haven and refuge
Gentle words of kindness fall from your lips
Your hands are filled with mercy
They are the ones that I'll long to hold
Your voice will be one of peace
And your presence will put me at ease

Scars

The Best
....

With my head on your shoulder, or resting on your chest
Tucked beneath your arm feels the best

Marina Murray

Be My Rock

Your peaceful voice comforts,
the wild pieces of my soul.

Lost with You

Let's get lost together
I don't care if we take one bike or two
Let's get lost together
A twisty, windy back road will do
Let's get lost together
And enjoy the wind and sun
Let's get lost together
It will be so much fun

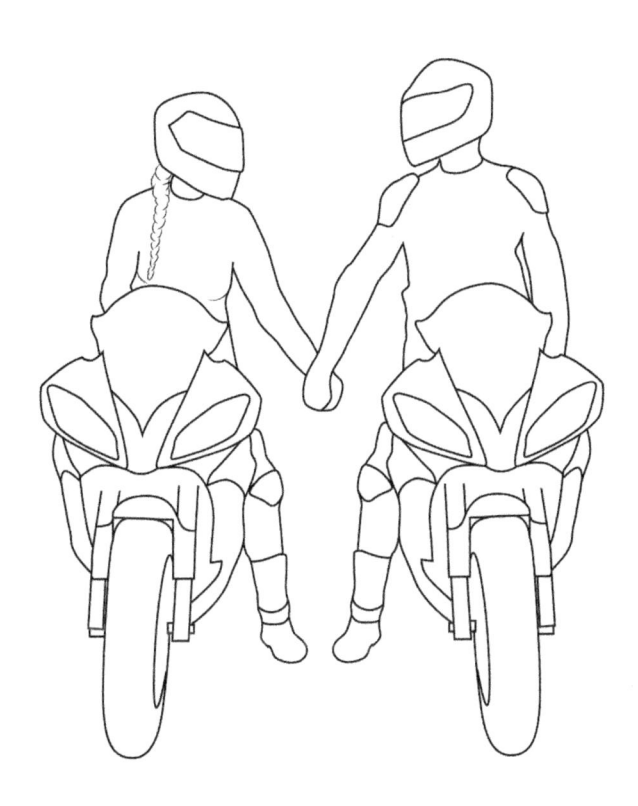

Marina Murray

Someplace with You

A dingy diner, or a candlelit dinner for two.
It doesn't really matter as long as it's someplace with you.

You

You'll be the reason behind my smile,
and the sparkle in my eyes.

Marina Murray

A Moment with You

I fell in love with your smile, and the
way that you look into my eyes.
As we sip our coffee and watch the sunrise
We enjoy the aroma of the roast
Simple moments like these mean the most

Scars

Your Song

Your light will be bright, but it will
still allow mine to shine
And the song of your soul will have a
tune that complements mine

Marina Murray

Dear Future Husband

I'm shy, so I probably won't say hi
Even though you caught my eye
I won't know what to say
So, I'll smile and look your way
You're a handsome guy
I really hope that you stop by
Wait, before you go
As your future wife, there are a few
things that you should know
I love it when you take me out on a date
I'll do my best not to make us late
I just want to look my best for you
That's why I am putting on outfit number two
I am a sucker for romance
So, every once in a while, pull me into
the kitchen to slow dance
I know that sometimes we will get
into an argument or fight
But I still want you to kiss me good night
Sometimes I try to be tough, and I'll say, "I'm ok."
But I really need you to hug me anyway
When problems come our way
Hold my hand when you pray
I'm always cold, especially my feet
So, I'll want to cuddle and listen to your heartbeat
When I've had a hard day
I need you to hug me and say, "It will be ok."
I hope that you read your Bible each day

And get on your knees when you pray
Your Bible will have highlights, notes, and
tear-stained pages just like mine.
And you'll be submitted to the God who is divine
I'll be the faithful partner that sticks by your side
And the Holy Spirit will be our guide
I'll cheer and scream
When we watch your favorite team
I'll wear your jersey when they play
Because I look better in it anyway
You buy me flowers once in a while
It always makes me smile
I love it when you run your fingers through my hair
These small gestures remind me that you care
I love it when you lead our family in prayer
And teach our kids how to share
You'll teach our son how to lead in love
And how to surrender to the God above
You'll teach our daughter how to pray
And you'll remind her that God has the final say
I'll need you every day
Even when we are old and gray
I'll be sure to say
That I love you each day
Please hurry, don't make me wait
I'm excited for our first date

Milton Keynes UK
Ingram Content Group UK Ltd.
UKHW010003020324
438623UK00004B/252